Our World

Our feelings

from happy to sad

Monica Hughes

Heinemann
LIBRARY

Little Nippers

www.heinemann.co.uk/library

Visit our website to find out more information about **Heinemann Library** books.

To order:
- ☎ Phone 44 (0) 1865 888066
- 🗎 Send a fax to 44 (0) 1865 314091
- 🖥 Visit the Heinemann Bookshop at www.heinemann.co.uk/library to browse our catalogue and order online.

First published in Great Britain by Heinemann Library, Halley Court, Jordan Hill, Oxford OX2 8EJ, part of Harcourt Education. Heinemann is a registered trademark of Harcourt Education Ltd.

Editorial: Jilly Attwood and Claire Throp
Design: Jo Hinton-Malivoire and bigtop, Bicester, UK
Models made by: Jo Brooker
Picture Research: Catherine Bevan
Production: Lorraine Warner

Originated by Dot Gradations
Printed and bound in China by South China Printing Company

ISBN 0 431 16252 2 (hardback)
06 05 04 03 02
10 9 8 7 6 5 4 3 2 1

ISBN 0 431 16257 3 (paperback)
06 05 04 03 02
10 9 8 7 6 5 4 3 2 1

British Library Cataloguing in Publication Data
Hughes, Monica
Our feelings
152.4
A full catalogue record for this book is available from the British Library.

Acknowledgements
The publishers would like to thank the following for permission to reproduce photographs:
Tudor Photography pp. **4**, **5**, **9**, **10**, **13**, **14**, **16**, **17**, **18**, **19**, **21**; Trevor Clifford p. **6**; Photodisc p. **7**; Corbis p. **8**; Eyewire p.**9**; Lupe Cuhna p. **15**; Bubbles p. **11** (Frans Rombout), p. **20** (Rebecca Lacey); Angela Hampton pp. **12**, **22**; Taxi p. **23**.

Cover photograph reproduced with permission of Bananastock.

The publishers would like to thank Annie Davy for her assistance in the preparation of this book.

Every effort has been made to contact copyright holders of any material reproduced in this book. Any omissions will be rectified in subsequent printings if notice is given to the publishers.

Contents

Happy and sad

Cameron is happy. He is smiling.
Do you feel happy when you smile?

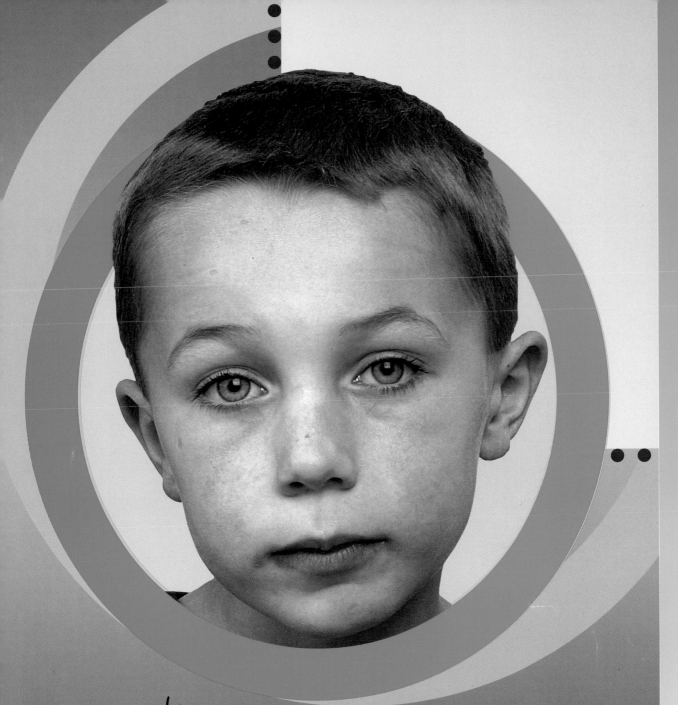

What do you think has
made Cameron sad?

Cold

Brrrr!

When you are cold
how do you get warm?

Hot

Phew!

How can these children cool down?

Tired

Jamie is tired!

Yawn!

What do you do when you are tired or sleepy?

Poor Polly. She has been sick.

How do you feel when you are sick or ill?

Excited

Rosie is very excited about her presents.

What's inside the parcels?

Paula is very excited because she is playing in the pool.

Sorry

Kim is sorry that she scribbled on the wall.

Jamie has broken a china cat.
It was an accident and he is very sorry.

Frightened

Joe was frightened because he had a bad dream.

He's all right now.

Claire is frightened of the dog.

When do you feel frightened?

Angry

Why do you
think Zara
is angry?

When Manjit is angry he punches a cushion. Then he feels much better!

Proud

James and Damon are proud of their pictures.

When have you felt proud of something you have done?

Index

The end

Notes for adults

This series supports the child's knowledge and understanding of their world, in particular their personal, social and emotional development area. The following Early Learning Goals are relevant to the series:
• respond to significant experiences, showing a range of feelings when appropriate
• have a developing awareness of their own needs, views and feelings and be sensitive to the needs and feelings of others
• have a developing respect for their own cultures and beliefs and those of other people.

This book explores a range of different feelings, many of which will be familiar to the child. The child can identify the feelings of the children in the book and compare these with their own experiences. Young children often have very powerful emotions and it can sometimes be useful to identify what factors lead to different feelings, and alternative ways of dealing with them. This can be encouraged by asking open-ended questions like: Why do you think she is frightened? Or how would you show you were sorry?

The series will help the child extend their vocabulary. Synonyms of words used in **Our Feelings** include *thrilled, disappointed, frozen, boiling, exhausted, excited, regret, scared, terrified, annoyed* and *honoured*. Words that describe the face include *smile, laugh, frown* and *scowl*.

The following additional information about our feelings may be of interest: It takes more muscles to frown than it does to smile! Some feelings are related to physical needs like thirst, hunger and cold. Others concern the emotions. Human beings have both kinds and so do many animals – think of cats when they are frightened and dogs when they are pleased.

Follow-up activities

Think of other verses (using different feelings and actions) for 'If you are happy and you know it'. Play 'Guess how I am feeling' by making different faces.